Explore the Solar System

Human Space Exploration

WORLD
BOOK

a Scott Fetzer company
Chicago
www.worldbookonline.com

World Book, Inc.
233 N. Michigan Avenue
Chicago, IL 60601
U.S.A.

For information about other World Book publications, visit our Web site at **http://www.worldbookonline.com** or call **1-800-WORLDBK (967-5325)**.

For information about sales to schools and libraries, call **1-800-975-3250 (United States)**, or **1-800-837-5365 (Canada)**.

Library of Congress Cataloging-in-Publication data
Human space exploration.
    p. cm. -- (Explore the solar system)
   Summary: "An introduction to human space exploration for primary and intermediate grade students, with information about the early history of space travel and current space exploration. Includes a list of highlights for each chapter, fun facts, glossary, resource list, and index" -- Provided by publisher.
   Includes index.
   ISBN 978-0-7166-9543-1
   1. Space probes--Juvenile literature. 2. Manned space flight--Juvenile literature. 3. Outer space--Exploration--Juvenile literature. I. World Book, Inc.
   TL793.H793 2011
   629.45--dc22
                        2010009002

ISBN 978-0-7166-9533-2 (set)
Printed in China by Leo Paper Products Ltd.,
   Heshan, Guangdong
1st printing August 2010

Staff
Executive Committee
Vice President and Chief Financial Officer:
   Donald D. Keller
Vice President and Editor in Chief: Paul A. Kobasa
Vice President, Licensing & Business Development:
   Richard Flower
Chief Technology Officer: Tim Hardy
Managing Director, International: Benjamin Hinton
Director, Human Resources: Bev Ecker

Editorial:
Associate Director, Supplementary Publications:
   Scott Thomas
Managing Editor, Supplementary Publications:
   Barbara A. Mayes
Senior Editor, Supplementary Publications:
   Kristina A. Vaicikonis
Manager, Research, Supplementary Publications:
   Cheryl Graham
Manager, Contracts & Compliance
   (Rights & Permissions): Loranne K. Shields
Editor: Michael DuRoss
Writer: Karen Ingebretsen
Indexer: David Pofelski

Graphics and Design:
Manager: Tom Evans
Coordinator, Design Development
   and Production: Brenda B. Tropinski
Designer: Matt Carrington
Contributing Photographs Editor: Carol Parden

Pre-Press and Manufacturing:
Director: Carma Fazio
Manufacturing Manager: Steven K. Hueppchen
Production/Technology Manager: Anne Fritzinger
Proofreader: Emilie Schrage

Picture Acknowledgments:
Cover front: NASA Human Spaceflight Collection;
Cover back: NASA/JPL-Caltech/UCLA.

© Alamy Images 53; APImages/NASA 15; APWorldwide 57; Bio Serve Space Tech/University of Colorado 27; © Corbis 9, 59; Esther C. Goddard 7; JPL 7; NASA 1, 4, 9, 10, 12, 15, 16, 17, 18, 19, 20, 22, 23, 24, 27, 29, 31, 32, 33, 34, 35, 36, 37, 38, 40, 42, 45, 47, 48, 51, 53; NASATV 27; © PhotoEdit 54; Scaled Composites 57; Shutterstock 53

Astronomers use different kinds of photos to learn about such objects in space as planets. Many photos show an object's natural color. Other photos use false colors. Some false-color images show types of light the human eye cannot normally see. Others have colors that were changed to highlight important features. When appropriate, the captions in this book state whether a photo uses natural or false color.

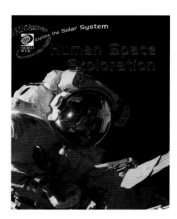

Cover image:
An astronaut updates communication equipment outside the International Space Station.

Contents

If a word is printed in **bold letters that look like this,** that word's meaning is given in the glossary on pages 60-61.

Where Does Space Begin?

There is no clear boundary between the **atmosphere** of Earth and outer space. The farther you go from Earth's surface, the thinner the air gets. But most scientists say that outer space begins about 60 miles (95 kilometers) above Earth. Many countries have agreed that the **Karman Line,** an imaginary boundary about 62 miles (100 kilometers) above Earth's surface, is the start of outer space.

When human beings decided to travel into space, they chose Earth's **moon** as the first place to visit. This made sense, because the moon is much closer to Earth than any of the **planets** in the **solar system.** It takes less fuel and time to reach the moon than other objects in space. The moon is about 238,897 miles (384,467 kilometers) from Earth. By comparison, Venus—the planet closest to Earth—is about 23.7 million miles (38.2 million kilometers) away. Neptune, the outermost planet in the solar system, is more than 2.7 billion miles (4.3 billion kilometers) away.

Highlights

- There is no clear boundary between Earth's atmosphere and outer space.
- Most scientists agree that space begins about 60 miles (95 kilometers) above Earth.
- Many countries consider the Karman Line to mark the beginning of outer space.

The Karman Line marks the boundary
between Earth's atmosphere and outer space.

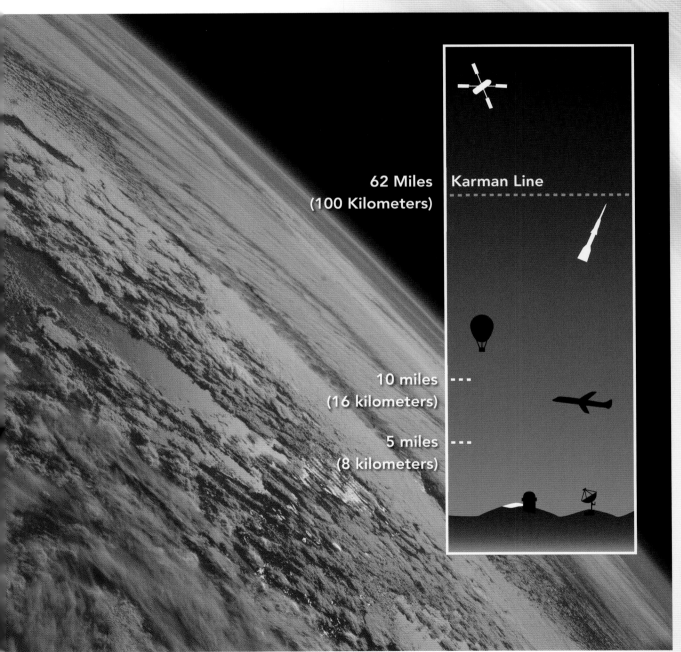

62 Miles | Karman Line
(100 Kilometers)

10 miles - - -
(16 kilometers)

5 miles - - -
(8 kilometers)

What Were the First Probes Launched into Space?

In the 1930's, scientists began to build and test **rockets** that they hoped would one day be used for space travel. Starting in about 1955, other scientists developed artificial **satellites** that were to be launched into space using rockets.

In 1957, the Soviet Union launched the first artificial satellite. The Soviet Union was a powerful country that existed from 1922 to 1991. The Soviet satellite, called Sputnik *(SPUHT nihk),* had no **astronauts** on board. Unpiloted satellites were a way of learning more about space before sending human beings there. The Soviet Union was also the first country to launch a **probe** to the surface of the **moon.** That probe, Luna 2, was launched in 1959.

Fun Fact

Vanguard I, the first satellite successfully launched by the United States, has been orbiting Earth for more than 50 years since its launch in 1958.

Highlights

- The Soviet Union launched the first artificial satellite, called Sputnik, in 1957.
- The first U.S. satellites to be launched successfully were Explorer 1 and Vanguard 1 in 1958.
- The first probe to the surface of the moon, Luna 2, was launched by the Soviet Union in 1959.

The first satellites that the United States launched successfully were Explorer 1 and Vanguard 1. They were launched in 1958. Vanguard 1 is still in **orbit** today. This satellite has sent a lot of information to Earth. Some of its data proved that Earth is slightly pear-shaped, not perfectly round. This information has helped map makers make more accurate world maps.

A team of scientists, including physicist James Van Allen (center) and rocket pioneer Wernher von Braun (right), hold a model of Explorer 1, which was successfully launched on Jan. 31, 1958.

American rocket pioneer Robert H. Goddard (left) and his assistants work on an early rocket in 1940.

What Was the "Space Race"?

In the late 1950's and early 1960's, the United States and the Soviet Union were political rivals. Both countries were working on space exploration programs at that time. The Soviet Union's launch of the **satellite** Sputnik (later called Sputnik 1) in 1957 surprised America. U.S. leaders vowed to do whatever was needed to catch up. This was the start of the **space race.**

Soon after, the U.S. National Aeronautics and Space Administration (NASA) was founded. This agency gathered researchers and laboratories, allowing people to work together toward the goal of space exploration. NASA played a key role in the eventual success of the American space program.

The space race faded by the 1970's, when both the United States and the Soviet Union began to pursue other goals in space. Today, many nations work together on projects in space, including the International Space Station, (ISS—see page 48). Both Russia, which was once part of the Soviet Union, and the United States helped to build the ISS.

Highlights

- The space race was a time of competition between the United States and the Soviet Union over which country would be the first to achieve important goals in exploring outer space.
- The space agency NASA was formed to help the United States achieve its goals.
- Today, many countries work together on space projects.

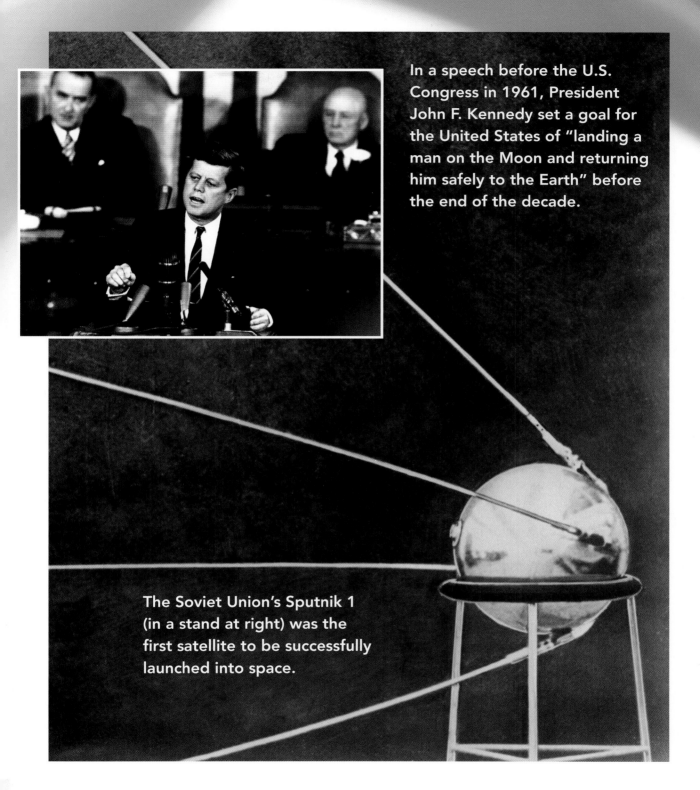

In a speech before the U.S. Congress in 1961, President John F. Kennedy set a goal for the United States of "landing a man on the Moon and returning him safely to the Earth" before the end of the decade.

The Soviet Union's Sputnik 1 (in a stand at right) was the first satellite to be successfully launched into space.

What Were the First Piloted Spacecraft Like?

U.S. astronaut Walter M. Schirra, Jr., is helped into a Mercury capsule before his flight into space in 1962.

The very first piloted spacecraft had room for only one person. That spacecraft was the Soviet Union's Vostok. The Vostok was designed to fall onto land with a parachute. The first type of piloted spacecraft designed by the United States—the Mercury spacecraft—was designed to land in the ocean.

As space programs continued, the **capsules** in which the **astronauts** sat were made bigger so that two or more people could

- The Soviet Union's first capsule, Vostok, was made to land with a parachute.
- The first U.S. capsule, Mercury, was made to land in the ocean.
- The earliest space capsules carried only one person. Later capsules carried two or more people.

The Soviet Vostok capsule

The U.S. Mercury capsule

travel on a flight. These capsules were also able to carry more supplies so that astronauts could stay in space longer. The first spacecraft could stay in space for only about a day. But soon spacecraft could remain in space for up to two weeks.

American spacecraft have sometimes been changed because of comments from the astronauts. For example, astronauts asked for a larger window on an early Mercury capsule, and NASA agreed.

The escape **hatch** was also redesigned. In 1967, three astronauts died in a fire on Apollo 1. The capsule's hatch took 90 seconds to open. NASA made new hatch that could be opened in just a few seconds.

What Gives a Spacecraft the Power for Liftoff?

Overcoming **gravity** is a spacecraft's biggest challenge. A powerful **rocket** called a **launch vehicle** helps a spacecraft overcome gravity and reach space.

Rockets burn either liquid or solid fuel. This fuel is combined with a substance called an oxidizer *(OK suh DY zuhr)*. An oxidizer adds the **oxygen** that fuel needs to burn in space, where there is no air.

Rockets are made up of stages, or sections. Each stage falls away after it is used up, so that the rest of the spacecraft is lighter. Releasing unneeded stages helps the spacecraft use less fuel as it continues in space.

Sometimes rockets called **boosters** are attached to the launch vehicle. Boosters help especially heavy spacecraft overcome gravity.

Highlights

- In order for a spacecraft to lift off, it must overcome the force of gravity.
- Rockets called launch vehicles help spacecraft to lift off.
- Launch vehicles may carry either solid or liquid fuel.
- Large, heavy spacecraft may also need booster rockets.

The space shuttle Discovery is carried into space by a launch vehicle with two boosters. The external tank (orange) is a rocket that carries liquid fuel. The boosters strapped to its sides (only one is visible in the photo) carry solid fuel.

Is Space Exploration Dangerous?

Space exploration has many dangers. Tragic accidents have taken the lives of U.S. **astronauts** as well as **cosmonauts** in the Soviet space program.

Scientists can take action in advance to reduce some of the risks of traveling or living in space. Double *hulls* (the outer walls of a spacecraft) protect against damage caused by *micrometeoroids* (dust particles) and *debris* (space trash). Filters on the windows of a spacecraft protect against damaging **ultraviolet rays** from the sun. Heat shields and a thermal-control system keep people inside the craft safe from the extreme heat and cold of space.

Other risks are harder to predict. Spacecraft are complex vehicles, and it is not always possible to know how something may go wrong. When an explosion occurred on the Apollo 13 spacecraft in 1970, only the fast thinking of the crew in space and NASA scientists on the ground saved the spacecraft and enabled the astronauts to return safely to Earth.

Highlights

- Both U.S. astronauts and Soviet cosmonauts have died during space exploration.
- Scientists who build spacecraft try to make them strong and safe, but sometimes unexpected dangers arise.

Fun Fact

Since 1957, more than 13,000 objects larger than 4 inches (10 centimeters) have begun to orbit Earth as space trash. These fast-moving objects are a serious danger to spacecraft.

A U.S. naval crew recovers the damaged Apollo 13 spacecraft at sea (above). The bottom of the space shuttle (right) is inspected during each mission for signs of damage to the tiny tiles that protect the spacecraft from the intense heat of launch and landing.

What Is Microgravity and How Does It Affect Space Travel?

Astronauts are frequently shown floating aboard a spacecraft in what is often called "zero **gravity**" or weightlessness. Zero gravity is actually **microgravity,** a state of extremely low gravity. During space flights, microgravity affects both astronauts and their spacecraft.

U.S. astronaut Leland Melvin aboard the space shuttle Atlantis watches his food, a pair of scissors, and a spoon float by in the microgravity of space.

16 Explore the Solar System

Microgravity affects the human body in many ways. In the first few days of a mission, about half of all space travelers experience "space sickness." Travelers feel confused—like they are always upside down, no matter which way they turn. They may become sick and vomit. Medicines can help them feel better, and the condition usually goes away after a few days. Other effects on the body include a muscle weakness known as deconditioning.

Microgravity affects a spacecraft just as much as it does the astronauts. In a microgravity environment, fuel does not drain from tanks, so it must be squeezed out by high-pressure gas. Hot air does not rise in microgravity, so fans must be used to circulate the air.

Highlights

- Although many people think there is no gravity in space, there is actually a little gravity, or a state of microgravity.
- Microgravity can make astronauts feel sick in space and make spacecraft harder to operate.
- There are things scientists can do to make astronauts feel better and spacecraft work better in microgravity.

United States astronaut Sandra Magnus exercises aboard the International Space Station to keep her muscles from growing weak while she is in space.

Who Were the First People to Travel in Space?

Soviet cosmonaut Yuri Gagarin travels to the launchpad on April 12, 1961. Gagarin was the first person to travel in space.

Highlights

- Soviet cosmonaut Yuri Gagarin was the first person to travel in space, in April 1961.
- Astronaut Alan B. Shepard, Jr., was the first American to travel in space, in May 1961.
- A dog and a chimpanzee traveled in space even before human beings did.

A **cosmonaut** from the Soviet Union named Yuri Gagarin *(YOOR ee gah GAHR ihn)* was the first person to travel in space. He **orbited** Earth on April 12, 1961, in a trip that lasted 1 hour and 48 minutes. After the flight, he returned safely to Earth.

The first American in space was Alan B. Shepard, Jr. On May 5, 1961, he **rocketed** 117 miles (188 kilometers) into space and landed back on Earth 15 minutes later.

Astronaut Alan B. Shepard, Jr., enters his Mercury capsule as he prepares to become the first American in space.

But even before human beings first explored space, animals traveled on spacecraft. An 11-pound (5-kilogram) dog named Laika *(LY kuh)* was the first space passenger. Laika flew aboard the Soviet craft Sputnik 2 in 1957. Other animal passengers included a chimpanzee named Ham, who made a 16-minute flight in a U.S. Mercury **capsule** in 1961. Over the years, space flights have also included bees, fish, frogs, mice, snails, and other animals.

Who Was the First Person to Walk in Space? To Walk on the Moon?

Soviet **cosmonaut** Alexei Leonov *(uh lyih KSYAY lee OH nohf)* became the first person to step outside a spacecraft and float freely in space. This first **extravehicular activity** took place on March 18, 1965. But the historic event almost ended in disaster. When Leonov tried to get back inside the space-craft, he found that his spacesuit had *inflated* (filled with air) so much that he could not bend his body to enter the opening to the **airlock.** Finally, he was able to release enough air from his suit to get back onboard Voshkod 2.

United States **astronaut** Neil A. Armstrong was the first person to walk on the surface of the **moon.** After taking the first step on its barren landscape on July 20, 1969, he spoke the now-famous words, "That's one small step for a man, one giant leap for mankind."

- Soviet cosmonaut Alexei Leonov was the first person to walk in space, in 1965.
- U.S. astronaut Neil A. Armstrong was the first person to walk on the moon, in 1969.

Neil Armstrong stands beside the lunar module (landing craft) after becoming the first person to walk on the moon. He planted the U.S. flag on the lunar surface.

Cosmonaut Alexei Leonov (in a series of photographs above) became the first person to walk in space.

What Did Astronauts Take from the Moon? Leave on the Moon?

During all six Apollo **moon** landings, **astronauts** collected rock and soil samples to take back to Earth for study. Altogether, astronauts gathered about 840 pounds (384 kilograms) of samples. Some moon rocks are on display in the National Museum of Natural History in Washington, D.C., and in several other U.S. museums. A small number of rocks were given to other countries as goodwill gifts. Most of the

Highlights

- The Apollo astronauts left a flag and a plaque on the moon in 1969.
- Footprints left by astronauts on the moon will probably remain for millions of years.
- Many spacecraft have also been left on the moon, either accidentally or deliberately.

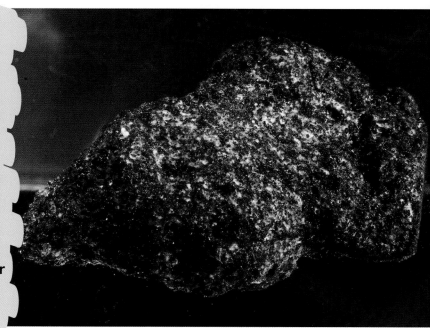

A moon rock brought back by Apollo astronauts

material returned by the Apollo missions is stored in NASA vaults.

Many more objects were left on the moon than were taken away. Astronauts Neil Armstrong and Buzz Aldrin planted a U.S. flag on the moon during their first moonwalk, on July 20, 1969. They also left a plaque. And, of course, all of the astronauts left their footprints. Because there is no wind or water on the moon to disturb them, the footprints should last for millions of years.

The largest objects left on the moon are *stages* (sections) of **rockets** and spacecraft from various countries. These objects either crashed into the moon accidentally or were deliberately crashed during missions exploring the moon. Scientists estimate that about 388,000 pounds (176,000 kilograms) of debris has been left on the moon.

A U.S. flag (above) and a plaque (below) were left on the moon by astronauts Neil Armstrong and Buzz Aldrin in 1969. Their footprints are also visible below the flag.

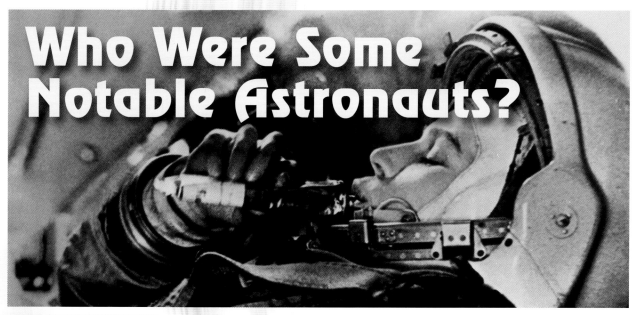

Who Were Some Notable Astronauts?

First woman in space, Soviet cosmonaut Valentina Tereshkova (1963)

First Canadian astronaut, Marc Garneau (1984)

First African-American astronaut, Guion S. Bluford, Jr. (1983)

First Hispanic-American astronaut, Franklin Chang-Diaz (1986)

First American woman in space, astronaut Sally Ride (1983)

First Australian astronaut, Andy Thomas (1996)

People who made history by traveling in space include Valentina Tereshkova (*VAH lehn TEE nah teh rehsh KAW vah*). Tereshkova, a Soviet **cosmonaut,** was the first woman in space. She made the flight in Vostok 6 in June 1963. The first U.S. woman in space was Sally K. Ride. She and four other **astronauts,** made a six-day flight on the space shuttle Challenger in June 1983.

In a flight aboard Challenger, in August 1983, Guion S. Bluford, Jr., became the first African American to go into space. In September 1992, on the space shuttle Endeavour, Mae C. Jemison became the first African American woman to do so.

The youngest astronaut to travel in space was Soviet cosmonaut Gherman Titov (*GUR men TEE tohf*). He was 25 years old when he piloted Vostok 2 in August 1961. The oldest was retired astronaut John H. Glenn, who, in 1998, flew aboard the space shuttle Discovery. Glenn was 77 years old at that time.

The first Canadian in space was Marc Garneau, on the space shuttle Challenger in 1984.

Highlights

- The first women in space were Soviet cosmonaut Valentina Tereshkova in 1963 and American astronaut Sally K. Ride in 1983.
- The youngest astronaut was Soviet cosmonaut Gherman Titov, who was 25. The oldest was retired U.S. astronaut John Glenn, who was 77.

What Kinds of Scientific Experiments Have Been Carried Out in Space?

Many of the experiments performed in space have focused on the effects of **microgravity** on animals, plants, and people. Other experiments have explored the properties of various *materials* (solid forms of matter) in space.

United States scientists began performing experiments in space aboard Skylab, the first American space station. It was in orbit from 1973 to 1979. Spacelab, a reusable laboratory, traveled in the cargo bay of NASA's space shuttles on various missions from 1983 to 1997. There, scientists conducted experiments in such fields as astronomy, biology, and medicine.

Scientists from various nations have also conducted experiments aboard the International Space Station. Sometimes, students are involved in the experiments. In 2008, students compared the lifecycles of butterflies in space with those on Earth.

Highlights

- One of the main types of experiments scientists perform in space is to observe the effects of microgravity on plants, animals, and people.
- Scientists also study whether the properties of various materials change in space.
- Sometimes students participate in space experiments, too.

Astronaut James D. van Hoften
studies a bee experiment aboard
the space shuttle Challenger in 1984.

Orb weaver spiders in an experiment aboard the International Space Station
in 2008 at first were able to weave only a tangled web (below, left). But after
a few days, they became used to the microgravity conditions of space and
wove the symmetrical web they are known for (below, right).

What Is the Space Shuttle Like?

The space shuttle system is made up of three parts: (1) an **orbiter,** (2) an external fuel tank, and (3) two solid rocket **boosters.** The *nose* (front) of the orbiter contains the crew cabin. As many as seven **astronauts** typically live and work in the cabin.

From the **flight deck** at the front of the orbiter, the pilot can look through the front and side windows. The middeck, under the flight deck, has more seats, equipment lockers, sleeping facilities, and a toilet compartment. The shuttle's "kitchen" includes hot- and cold-water dispensers, an oven, serving trays for food, and a water heater, but no freezer or refrigerator. The payload bay holds the cargo, or goods, hauled by the shuttle. The engines are in the orbiter's tail.

The space shuttle was the first reusable spacecraft. To be reusable, it had to land on solid ground, not water. So the shuttle was designed to take off like a **rocket** but land like an airplane. A heat shield allows the shuttle to withstand many reentries into Earth's **atmosphere.**

The shuttle flew its first mission in 1981. NASA planned to end space shuttle missions by 2011.

Highlights

- The space shuttle was the first reusable spacecraft.
- It flew its first mission in 1981.
- NASA planned to end space shuttle missions by 2011.

Parts of the space shuttle system

Rocket booster

Fuel tank

Rocket booster

Orbiter

The space shuttle Discovery is prepared for launch.

What Do Astronauts Eat in Space?

The food served on a spacecraft has come a long way since the Mercury **astronauts** dined in space. Those early astronauts had to squeeze their semiliquid foods—said to be less than tasty—out of aluminum tubes similar to toothpaste tubes.

Today, astronauts have many choices of things to eat, including macaroni and cheese, beef, peanut butter and jelly, chicken soup, brownies, apples, carrot sticks, and nuts. Some modern meals in space are ready-to-eat. The astronauts have to add water to other foods. Meals can be heated in an on-board oven.

All drinks, even coffee and cocoa, are served in a pouch with

Fun Fact

Astronauts in space eat a lot of wet and sticky foods, such as oatmeal, pudding, and stew. That is because such foods stick to a fork or spoon instead of breaking apart into crumbs and flying off.

a straw or in a squeeze bottle. That is because in **microgravity,** if you tip a cup, the liquid will not move toward your mouth. Instead, it will float away.

In space, astronauts can eat upside down—or at least upside down in relation to the spacecraft. That is because in microgravity, there is no true "up" or "down."

Russian cosmonaut Yuri Malenchenko (left) and U.S. astronaut Edward Lu prepare to eat a meal aboard the International Space Station in 2003.

Highlights

- Early astronauts had to squeeze their food out of tubes similar to those that hold toothpaste.

- Today, astronauts have much more variety in their meals.

- Most astronaut meals today are either ready-to-eat or prepared by adding water to them.

- Astronauts must drink all liquids—even coffee and cocoa—through a straw.

How Do Astronauts Stay Clean in Space?

There is no shower, bathtub, or sink on the space shuttle. Room and water are limited, and water floating around in **microgravity** could damage sensitive equipment. Shuttle **astronauts** "bathe" by rubbing wet cloths over their body, using one for washing and one for rinsing. They wash their hair with rinse-less shampoo. They brush their teeth using toothpaste that can be swallowed or regular toothpaste that is either spit into a

Highlights

- Astronauts aboard the space shuttle use washcloths and rinseless shampoo to stay clean.
- Astronauts aboard the space station can bathe in an enclosed, cylindrical shower and then vacuum up the water.

Astronaut Kenneth D. Cockrell washes his hair aboard the space shuttle Columbia. He uses a special shampoo that does not need to be rinsed out.

Cosmonaut Fyodor Yurchikhin cuts astronaut Sunita Williams's hair aboard the ISS. Williams holds a vacuum device to capture the bits of cut hair.

tissue or suctioned out, like in a dentist's office.

The International Space Station (ISS) has a *cylindrical* (tall and round) shower stall. Crew members close the door and spray themselves with water. Soap and water stick to the skin because of microgravity. When they are finished, crew members vacuum up the water. NASA's Skylab space station had a similar shower.

Astronauts on the space shuttle and the ISS use toilets that flush with air, not water. The toilets work like vacuum cleaners, with fans that suck air and waste into a storage tank. Astronauts must clamp themselves to the seat while using the toilet, to keep from floating away. In 2008, astronauts began recycling all the water aboard the space station so that it could be reused.

What Do Astronauts Wear on a Space Mission?

Crews on the space shuttle wear special suits for launch and reentry. They wear different suits for **extravehicular activity (EVA),** or work outside the spacecraft or space station. Launch and Entry Suits protect against fire and keep pressure around the **astronauts'** bodies in case the spacecraft's pressurization systems fail. EVA suits act like a self-contained spacecraft to keep the astronaut safe.

On the International Space Station, astronauts wear ordinary shorts or pants, a short- or long-sleeved shirt, and socks. The pants and shorts have plenty of

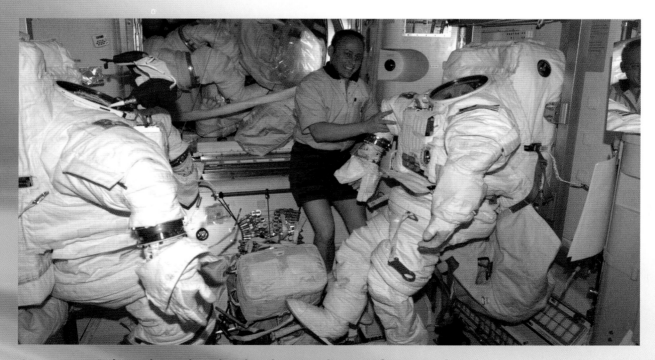

Astronaut Edward Fincke checks the condition of extravehicular activity (spacewalking) suits aboard the ISS.

A crew aboard the space shuttle Endeavour prepares for lift-off in their Launch and Entry Suits in 2002.

pockets with Velcro closings to secure objects that would otherwise float away. Astronauts wear the same type of clothing inside the shuttle, after launch and before reentry.

Crews on the shuttle carry a change of clothes for each day of the mission. On the ISS, there is no washing machine and little storage space, so astronauts change their shirts and pants about once every three or four days. Dirty clothing is usually placed in an unpiloted, one-way vehicle that has carried supplies to the station. The vehicle is placed on a collision course with Earth and burns up as it reenters Earth's **atmosphere.**

Highlights

- Astronauts wear one type of suit for launch and reentry and another type for spacewalks.
- Aboard the shuttle and the ISS, astronauts wear short- or long-sleeved shirts and pants or shorts with many pockets.

How Do Astronauts Sleep in Space?

On the International Space Station, there are small crew cabins, just big enough for one person. Each cabin has a sleeping bag and a window that looks out into space.

On the shuttle, there are no private rooms for crew members. Because of **microgravity**, shuttle **astronauts** could drift around the spacecraft as they sleep. So astronauts use sleeping bags that can be clipped to walls, the ceiling, or a seat. Or, they may decide to sleep strapped into the commander's or pilot's seats.

Astronaut Peggy Whitson slips into a sleeping compartment aboard the International Space Station.

All of these sleep choices prevent astronauts from bumping into one another or into equipment and walls that would wake or injure them. In microgravity, sleeping bags can be attached in any position that is practical. Since there is no "up" in space, the astronauts can sleep just as comfortably positioned *vertically* (up and down) as they can *horizontally* (side to side).

On the shuttle, astronauts may wear sleeping masks at bedtime to block the sunlight that streams in through the windows at times as the spacecraft **orbits** Earth.

A sleeping compartment aboard the ISS has places for astronauts to attach personal photos and their sleeping bag; a shelf or desktop to work on; and netted storage for clothing.

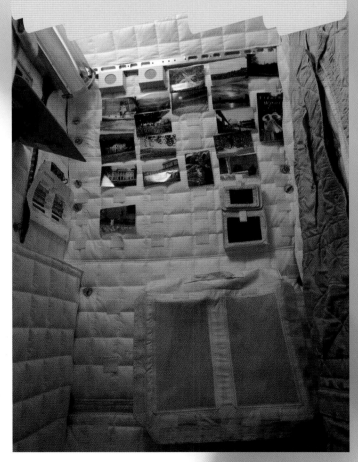

What Is the Space Shuttle Used For?

Space shuttles have carried artificial **satellites,** space **probes,** and other heavy loads into **orbit** around Earth since 1981. In addition, a shuttle can be used to retrieve artificial satellites that need repair. **Astronauts** aboard the shuttle can fix a satellite and then return it to orbit. Shuttle crews can also conduct many kinds of scientific experiments and observations.

In 1993, a crew from the shuttle Endeavour repaired the three-year-old orbiting Hubble Space Telescope. The repairs enabled the telescope to capture and send images in detail never seen before. Shuttles flew four other missions to Hubble over the years, the last one in 2009.

Shuttles also are used to take crews and cargo to and from the International Space Station. The shuttle Endeavour carried Unity, the first U.S.-built section of the space station, into orbit in 1998. Since then, shuttles have carried many other pieces of the station into space. They have also flown tons of supplies to the astronauts and experiments for scientists to conduct on the ISS.

Highlights

- The space shuttle flew its first mission in 1981.
- Space shuttles were scheduled to fly their last mission by 2011.
- Space shuttles have been used to carry heavy objects into space, repair satellites, and conduct experiments in microgravity.

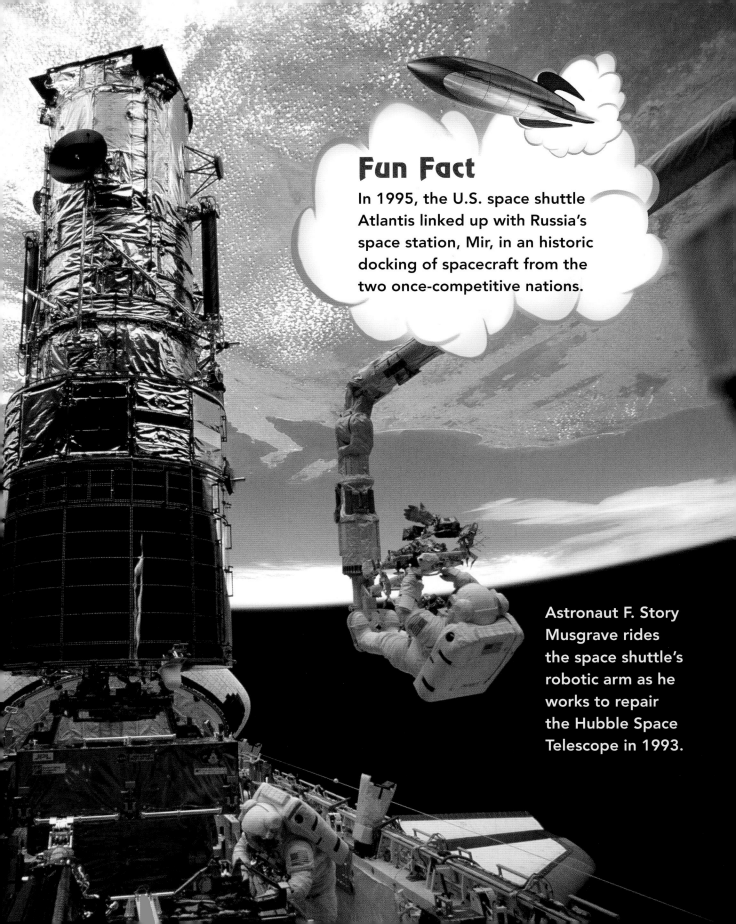

Fun Fact

In 1995, the U.S. space shuttle Atlantis linked up with Russia's space station, Mir, in an historic docking of spacecraft from the two once-competitive nations.

Astronaut F. Story Musgrave rides the space shuttle's robotic arm as he works to repair the Hubble Space Telescope in 1993.

How Do Astronauts Train for Shuttle Missions?

NASA has developed many tools to help **astronauts** train for missions in space. Many of these tools allow the crews to practice handling problems. If one of these problems arises during a mission, the crew is prepared to deal with it safely.

A device called the motion-based simulator enables astronauts to train in *launch* (taking off), *ascent* (going up), *reentry* (entering Earth's **atmosphere**), and landing. The device has a copy of the space shuttle **flight deck.** The simulator rocks, rolls, moves side-to-side, and vibrates just like the real shuttle **orbiter.**

Astronauts also practice in a fixed-base simulator. It has a replica of the flight deck and most of the middeck. Here, a crew trains for most of the tasks to be performed while in **orbit.**

To train for **extravehicular activity (EVA),** astronauts use the Neutral Buoyancy Laboratory. The laboratory, one of the world's largest indoor pools, simulates the **microgravity** condition that crews experience in space. Astronauts may also use a **gravity** simulator, to learn to walk and ride on the **moon** or Mars.

Highlights

- Astronauts train on simulators to learn launch, ascent, reentry, and landing procedures and how to perform tasks while in orbit.
- They train in a pool to learn to work outside a space vehicle.

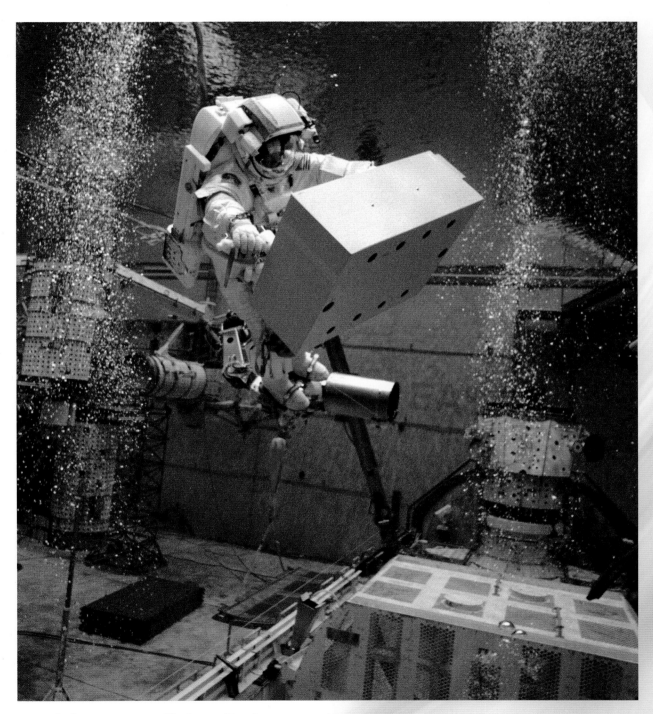

Swedish astronaut Christer Fuglesang trains in NASA's Neutral Buoyancy Laboratory, which imitates the microgravity conditions of space.

Who Manages the Shuttle from Earth?

Engineers at Mission Control at the Johnson Space Center in Houston monitor the space shuttle.

Ground preparations for a mission begin weeks or months before the launch date. Launch Control at the Kennedy Space Center in Florida is in charge of the shuttle all through preparation, until the message "tower clear" is announced. This message is broadcast a few seconds into the launch. It means that the shuttle has cleared the launch tower—the tower that holds and supports the craft in an upright position before take off—and has successfully launched. Then, Mission Control at the Johnson Space Center in Houston takes over. Mission Control remains in charge until the wheels stop when the **orbiter** has landed back on Earth.

Highlights

- A Launch Control group at the Kennedy Space Center in Florida is in charge of the shuttle until it clears the launch tower.
- Mission Control in Houston is in charge from the time the shuttle clears the tower until it lands.
- But the shuttle actually uses its own computers to fly into orbit and land.

Actually, the word "control" in the titles of both these groups is a little misleading. If everything is working as it should, no one—not even the **astronauts** on board—controls the shuttle during launch or reentry. The shuttle uses its own computers to fly into and out of **orbit.** Workers at Launch Control and Mission Control and the astronauts watch their monitors and step in if something is not working correctly.

Human Space Exploration **43**

What Will Replace the Space Shuttle?

The space shuttle was a step forward in the space program because it was the first spacecraft that was mostly reusable. Even so, some experts estimate that each mission costs $1 billion. Also, the **orbiters** are getting old.

Some experts also continue to raise safety concerns about the space shuttle. Two shuttle missions have ended in disaster. In 1986, the shuttle Challenger broke apart shortly after launch, and all seven **astronauts** aboard were killed. In 2003, the shuttle Columbia broke apart as it reentered Earth's **atmosphere.** All seven crew members died in this disaster, too.

For all these reasons, experts called for a new spacecraft to replace the shuttle. NASA hoped to

Fun Fact

Orion is the name of a constellation. It was also the name of the Apollo 16 Lunar Module, which carried astronauts to the surface of the moon in April 1972.

have a new craft, a **capsule** called Orion set atop a **rocket,** ready to fly by 2014. But in 2010, U.S. President Barack Obama called on private companies to build spacecraft to carry U.S. astronauts into space. Several companies were interested in doing so.

Until a new spacecraft becomes available, Russia's Soyuz spacecraft will carry U.S. astronauts to the space station. Russian and Japanese cargo vehicles will bring supplies to the station.

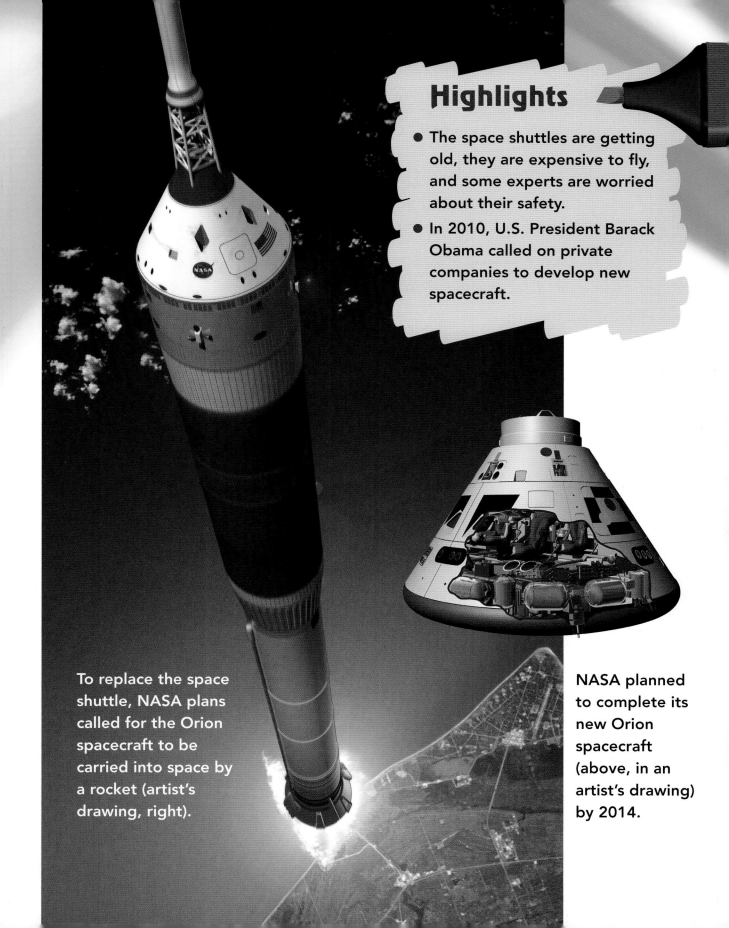

Highlights

- The space shuttles are getting old, they are expensive to fly, and some experts are worried about their safety.
- In 2010, U.S. President Barack Obama called on private companies to develop new spacecraft.

To replace the space shuttle, NASA plans called for the Orion spacecraft to be carried into space by a rocket (artist's drawing, right).

NASA planned to complete its new Orion spacecraft (above, in an artist's drawing) by 2014.

What Is a Space Station?

A space station is a place where people can live and work in space for long periods. One major reason to have a space station is so that the equipment can be carried into space only once. In addition, many **astronauts** can reuse a space station over time.

A space station **orbits** Earth, usually at about 200 to 300 miles (300 to 480 kilometers) above Earth's surface. A space station may serve as an observatory, laboratory, factory, workshop, warehouse, and fuel depot for refueling spacecraft.

Space stations are much larger than piloted spacecraft, so they provide more comforts. Piloted spacecraft may transport people between Earth and the space station. Unpiloted spacecraft may bring food, water, equipment—even mail— to the station.

The Soviet Union's Salyut 1, launched in 1971, was the first space station. It hosted a 23-day mission. Skylab, the first United States space station, was in orbit from 1973 through 1979. Mir was the longest-lived station, in orbit from 1986 to 2001. It was launched by the Soviet Union.

Highlights

- The first space station was the Soviet Union's Salyut 1.
- Skylab was the first U.S. space station.
- Space stations are places where people can live and work in space for long periods of time.

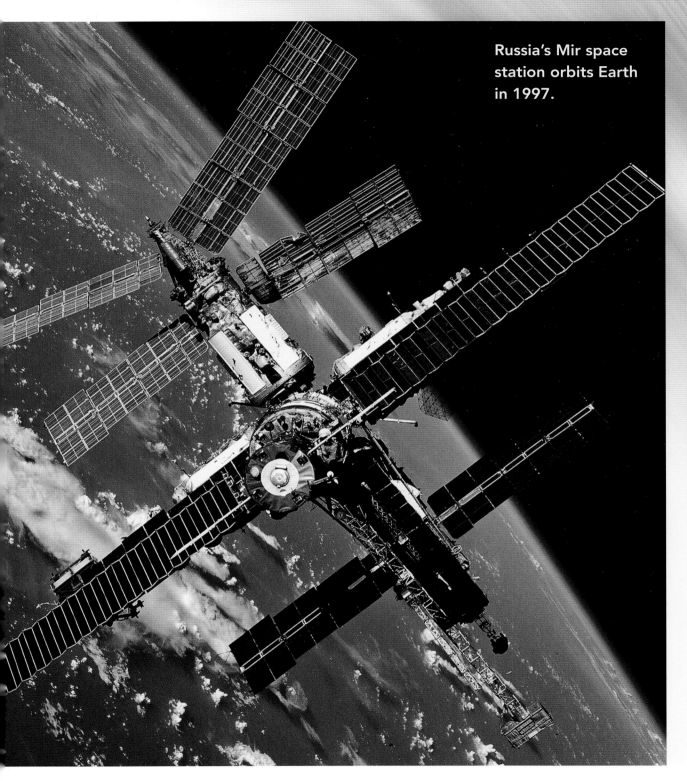

Russia's Mir space station orbits Earth in 1997.

What Is the International Space Station?

The International Space Station

Highlights

- The International Space Station is a joint project by more than 15 nations.
- Its first two pieces were the Russian-built Zarya and U.S.-built Unity modules.
- Construction of the station in space began in 1998.

The International Space Station is a large, inhabited Earth **satellite** being built in space. The station is being constructed in **modules,** or pieces. The first module, Zarya, was built and launched by Russia in 1998. The second, Unity, was built and launched by the United States later in 1998. As modules arrive in space, they are connected to the existing modules. When complete, the space station will consist of about eight main modules.

The space station is truly an international effort. More than 15 nations, including Canada, Russia, and the United States, are partners in the project. The joining of the Zarya and Unity modules symbolized the start of a new era in cooperation between nations in space exploration.

That cooperation became especially important in 2003 and 2004. At that time, safety concerns caused NASA to *ground* (refuse to let fly) the U.S. shuttle fleet. Russian Soyuz spacecraft carried supplies and **astronauts** to the station. NASA resumed space shuttle flights to the station in 2005.

What Have We Learned So Far on the International Space Station?

Ever since the first piloted space flights, scientists have studied the effects of space exposure and **microgravity** on the human body. **Astronauts** on the International Space Station (ISS) continue this research. It is even more important now that people spend months at a time in space. What we learn today may also be used on ultralong flights to other **planets.**

Astronauts on the ISS also carry out experiments with construction materials. They expose hundreds of possible future space construction materials to the environment of space. Then, samples are returned to Earth and studied. NASA hopes the results will help engineers build stronger, more durable spacecraft.

Astronauts are not the only people conducting research from the space station. A NASA program called Earth Knowledge Acquired by Middle School Students (EarthKAM) allows thousands of middle school students to photograph and study Earth, using a digital camera mounted on the ISS.

Cosmonaut Gennady Padalka measures the growth of plants in a greenhouse aboard the Zvezda module of the ISS as part of a biology experiment.

Highlights

- Scientists have tested how construction materials react to the environment of space.
- They have also measured the growth of various plants in space.
- Middle school students have also carried out experiments from the space station.

What Useful Things on Earth Were Created for the Space Program?

Many of the products people on Earth use every day are based on technology that was developed for NASA missions. For example, NASA developed the materials and technologies that are used in smoke

Highlights

- Many of the products we use today were developed by NASA scientists for use by astronauts.
- NASA technology has been used to make products in such fields as health and medicine, public safety, transportation, recreation, and computer technology.

Cordless tools were originally developed by NASA for use by the Apollo astronauts.

Technology developed by NASA has been used in such products as Tang breakfast drink, joystick controllers for video games, and ear thermometers.

European Space Agency astronaut Claude Nicollier uses a power tool during a mission to repair the Hubble Space Telescope in 1999.

detectors, ear thermometers, TV satellite dishes, joystick controllers for video games, transparent braces for teeth, and more shock-absorbent football helmets. Cordless tools also were developed by NASA to help Apollo astronauts drill for moon samples. Other NASA-related devices are being used in transportation, computer technology, and public safety.

How Can Kids Get Involved in Space Exploration ?

There are many ways that young people can get involved in space exploration. Boy Scout and Girl Scout organizations offer space-exploration achievement badges. To earn the badges, scouts learn about the history of space travel, design a base for the moon or Mars, or even build and launch model **rockets.**

NASA sponsors many programs for schools. In the "Send Your Art to Space" program, kids were invited to submit a piece of art that represented their school. That art was then sent to the International Space Station.

Fun Fact

Various nations use different names for their space explorers. U.S., Canadian, Australian, and European space explorers are called astronauts; Russian explorers, cosmonauts; Chinese, taikonauts; and explorers from India, vyomanauts.

With a personal computer, you can tune into NASA Direct—live webcasts leading up to every shuttle launch. These webcasts feature scientists, engineers, NASA managers, and **astronauts.** And during shuttle missions you can watch NASA TV on the Internet, with start-to-finish coverage from Mission Control.

Highlights

- Both Boy Scouts and Girl Scouts can earn merit badges by learning about space exploration.
- Many NASA programs allow students to play a part in specific space missions.
- Anyone with a computer can follow webcasts in which scientists and astronauts talk about their current mission.

A Cub Scout practices satellite repair on a simulator at NASA's Space Center in Houston.

Can Tourists Travel into Space?

Since the first piloted space flight in 1961, fewer than 1,000 people have flown in space. Even people who qualify as an **astronaut** are not guaranteed a mission. What other ways might there be to experience space travel and tourism in the future?

A few wealthy civilians have paid to travel to the International Space Station (ISS) aboard Russian spacecraft. The trips were arranged by Space Adventures, a private company. The company also offers **microgravity** training, simulated spacewalk training, simulator training on the Russian Soyuz spacecraft, and other programs.

The private British company Virgin Galactic began taking deposits in 2005 for brief flights into space on the VSS Enterprise (also called SpaceShipTwo). The company hoped to start flying tourists into space by around 2011.

Several other companies have developed plans for space hotels, including hotels on the **moon.** Who knows what will be next in space tourism? After all, not even the sky is the limit!

Highlights

- Fewer than 1,000 people have flown in space since the first piloted space flight in 1961.
- Several companies planned to carry tourists into space, allowing people who were not trained astronauts to experience microgravity and see Earth from space.

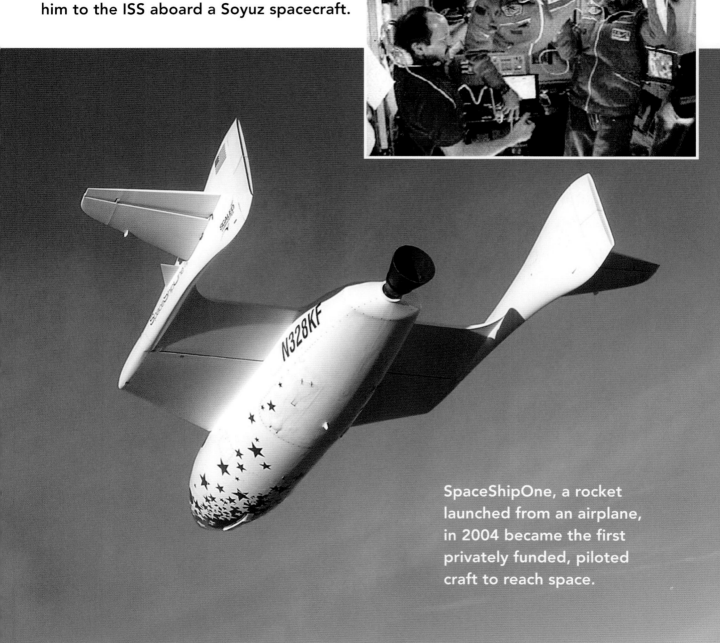

American multimillionaire Dennis Tito (right) enters the ISS in 2001. Tito became the first space tourist when he paid Russia a reported $20 million to fly him to the ISS aboard a Soyuz spacecraft.

SpaceShipOne, a rocket launched from an airplane, in 2004 became the first privately funded, piloted craft to reach space.

So You Want to Become a Space Explorer?

To become a NASA **astronaut,** you must have at least a bachelor's degree in engineering, science, or math. An advanced degree is even better. You also must have completed three years of related experience after graduation. Pilot astronauts must have at least 1,000 hours of experience in jet aircraft. Competition is extremely stiff. Usually, over 4,000 people apply for about 20 openings every two years.

Supporting the astronauts on every mission are many thousands of other workers, in jobs ranging from research pilots to microbiologists. Requirements for these vital positions vary, depending on the job.

Highlights

- To become a NASA astronaut, a candidate must have at least a bachelor's degree in engineering, science, or mathematics.
- Very few people become astronauts, and even fewer fly on a mission.
- But there are other ways students can experience being in space.

To experience a simulated space mission, some kids visit a Challenger Learning Center. About 50 centers—in Canada, South Korea, the United Kingdom, and the United States—offer scale models of mission control and an **orbiting** space station.

And for sheer fun, nothing beats space camp. At space camps in the United States, Canada, and Europe, kids may meet astronauts, try out motion and **microgravity** simulators, and design space robots.

A student tries out the cockpit of a simulated space shuttle at space camp.

Glossary

airlock On a spacecraft, the chamber between the outer door that leads to space and the door leading to the inside of the spacecraft.

astronaut A pilot or member of the crew of a spacecraft.

atmosphere The mass of gases that surrounds a planet.

booster A rocket sometimes attached to a launch vehicle to provide extra power.

capsule A section of a spacecraft that can be used or ejected as a unit.

cosmonaut A Russian astronaut.

extravehicular activity (EVA) Work or other activity outside a spacecraft.

flight deck The uppermost compartment of the cabin in a space shuttle, which contains the controls for the shuttle's guidance and navigation.

gravity The effect of a force of attraction that acts between all objects because of their mass (that is, the amount of matter the objects have).

hatch A door or opening on a spacecraft that can be sealed.

Karman Line An altitude of about 62 miles (100 kilometers) above Earth's surface (from sea level). This height has become an international boundary marking the beginning of outer space.

launch vehicle A rocket that carries a satellite or spacecraft into space.

microgravity A condition of very low gravity, especially approaching weightlessness.

module A self-contained unit in a spacecraft, designed to serve a particular function.

moon A smaller body that orbits a planet.

orbit The path that a smaller body takes around a larger body; for instance, the path that a planet takes around the sun. Also, to travel in an orbit.

orbiter In the space shuttle, a winged craft that looks like an airplane and which holds the cabin where the astronauts are.

oxygen A nonmetallic chemical element.

planet A large, round body in space that orbits a star. A planet must have sufficient gravitational pull to clear other objects from the area of its orbit.

probe An unpiloted device sent to explore space. Most probes send *data* (information) from space.

rocket A type of engine that pushes itself forward or upward by producing *thrust* (a force).

satellite A natural satellite is an object that orbits a planet or asteroid. An artificial satellite is an object built by people and launched into space, where it continuously orbits Earth or some other body. Artificial satellites are used to send weather or other scientific information back to Earth.

solar system A group of bodies in space made up of a star and the planets and other objects orbiting around the star.

ultraviolet rays An invisible form of light. The sun is the major natural source of ultraviolet rays on Earth.

For More Information

Books

Look to the Stars by Buzz Aldrin (G.P. Putnam's Sons, 2009)

Mission Control, This Is Apollo: The Story of the First Voyages to the Moon by Andrew Chaikin (Viking, 2009)

The Outer Limits: The Future of Space Exploration by Gary Miller (Gareth Stevens, 2010)

Space Exploration by Connie Jankowski (Compass Point Books, 2009)

Web sites

Curious About Astronomy? Ask an Astronomer
http://curious.astro.cornell.edu.space.php

NASA for Students
http://www.nasa.gov/audience/forstudents/index.html

NASA's Historical Archive
http://science.ksc.nasa.gov/history/history.html

Index